# Trauma in the Classroom

*Uncovering the Truth*

*About*

*Childhood Adversity*

Stacey L. Sly

STUDENT PHOTOS BY
ANGELA PEARSON

AUTHOR PHOTO BY
RANDY SLY

COVER DESIGN TEAM: RANDY & WALKER SLY

WITHDRAWN

1

SAGINAW CHIPPEWA ACADEMY
LIBRARY MEDIA CENTER
MT. PLEASANT, MI 48858

# Trauma in the Classroom

*Uncovering the Truth*

*About*

*Childhood Adversity*

Copyright © Stacey Sly, 2016

All rights reserved.

www.traumaintheclassroom.com

Published by:

WE are the Change, Ltd.

Las Vegas, Nevada

ISBN-13:978-0692711651

ISBN-10:0692711651

# CONTENTS

It is time for change.

This book is the result of countless hours of research. As a behavior interventionist for a school district, I noticed alarming trends and patterns in student behavior. The intensity of behavior was increasing, the age of the student was decreasing, and methods traditionally used to modify student behavior were not working. I felt helpless to provide teachers with real solutions. I wanted to know why our tried and true methods were not working on some kids, and what to do about it- and so the research began. While the students were playing *(or getting into trouble)* on their summer vacation, I was immersed in the literature. I took on the role of detective.

What I found was both incredible and hopeful. Incredible because the discourse of both biological science and social science are in perfect alignment. Teachers, social workers, psychologists, medical doctors, neuroscientists and developmental specialists all repeatedly confirm the same thing. **Childhood adversity hurts learning, and adversely shapes behavior in such a way, that children experiencing chronic adversity are incapable of responding to our typical interventions- either behavioral or academic.** There are stacks and stacks of literature on this topic, and decades of supporting research. Unlike other topics of research, with this topic, I have **NOT** found one single exception to the rule. The findings are substantiated time and time again, across all demographics and around the world.

My research also uncovered hope. There are proven methods to help these kids. <u>**All**</u> of the literature reports that healing, repair, and then learning are all possible.

Getting this information in the hands of educators is essential to getting these kids back on track. It is essential to ensuring the success of our future generations! The key is found in adequately expressing the magnitude of the problem and suitably demonstrating the ***power of change***.

This book brings supporting evidence from multiple sources together to both emphasize the enormity of this topic, and advocate for change in some of our current educational practices; change that both empowers the educator, and heals the child.

"BE THE **CHANGE**

YOU WANT TO

SEE IN **THE WORLD.**"

-MAHATMA GANDHI[1]

# 1

# THE EPIDEMIC

## --THE HIDDEN EPIDEMIC--

We have in our communities, a hidden epidemic. Most will not see it; some who do, will choose to ignore it. Those who recognize it are probably unaware of the magnitude of it. "Ignorance is bliss," after all. I used to be in this category, then I became a behavior interventionist. It became not only my job to recognize it, but also my job to fix it, or at least the symptoms of it. What is the hidden epidemic? On the surface, it is student behavior that is disruptive, severe, and harmful.

What kind of severe, disruptive and harmful behavior? On a typical day as a behavior interventionist, it is not unusual to respond to students who can dismantle a room in under five minutes, students who tip desks, tables and even throw chairs. It is not uncommon to respond to students who are self-injurious, or a physical threat to other students and adults. It is not uncommon to respond to students who are running from their classroom and even the school campus. Other student behaviors include: severe, sustained tantrum behavior with crying, kicking, crawling or rolling on the floor; students who attempt to hide from their peers and adults; students who refuse to come to class, stay in class, or work in class; and even students who sit silently and try not to draw any attention. The magnitude of these behaviors continues to increase year after year.

Sometimes behaviors of self-injury expand to self-harm. I have been called in to support young students with suicidal tendencies, even students as young as kindergarten. These are our community's children. We have to stop this epidemic! *We are their future!*

## --THE SOS--

Most believe these incidents are rare; I used to believe that too, but they are not. In 180 days of school, covering 20 schools, I will receive 75-100 new requests for student support. Recently, I met with several kindergarten teachers regarding their students who struggled to stay in class, who would bully and hurt their peers, hide in or under furniture and lacked basic skills of sitting, following directions, and interacting socially. The principal sent me this SOS one evening, "Please help! The kindergarten is running our school." During our meeting, there was an all-call for an older student who had not come back to class after lunch. His history includes violent, disruptive behaviors, and elopement (running away from the class or campus). These are just a few examples of students requiring additional assistance at this school.

Another elementary school had their greatest problem with the fifth grade. Roughly two-dozen fifth graders would frequently disrupt the learning environment. They would leave the class when they wanted, say what they wanted, and do what they wanted. On one occasion, when school police happened to be on campus, the principal asked him to go down and talk to this group. Instead of responding respectfully to his authority, a handful of those students verbally threatened him. Again, this is one example of what happened on one campus. These were not the only students requiring extraordinary intervention.

## --EXTRAORDINARY IMPACT --

The problem is not limited to the noticeable increase of students with these behaviors; it goes well beyond that. These kids are not able to fully benefit from their own education, but they are also interfering with the education of all other students on the campus. While adults work tirelessly to limit exposure of these disruptive behaviors, even if a student on the campus never sees them, he will still feel the impact simply because the number of adult resources required to manage these behaviors is extraordinary. It is also highly disproportionate. In order to keep these kids safe, and protect the safety of others, many adults often respond to one event, or spend much of their time supporting just a few students.

The reality is, while the number of students with these behaviors is on the rise, they still represent a very small percentage of the student population and therefore, supportive resources are limited. Schools often do not have designated adults to help these students, especially at the elementary level. Administrators are often pulled from other responsibilities, leaving them with less time to support, coach and mentor their teachers, build relationships with students and decreased opportunity to establish parent and community relationships.

## --THE WELL--

With violent, aggressive and severely disruptive behaviors on the rise, it raises the questions: *What is going on with these kids in this community? Is there a common thread? Is there something we need to address at the core of the problem? What are we missing?* Dr. Nadine Burke Harris delivered a TEDMED talk on this very issue. In her medical practice, she also recognized a "disturbing trend" among pediatric patients coming to see her: many with behavior problems.  Her philosophy?  "If you're a doctor, and you see a hundred kids that all drink from the same well, and ninety-eight of them develop diarrhea, you can go ahead and write the prescription for dose after dose of antibiotics, or you can walk over and say what the hell is in this well?"[2]  It was time to find out what was in the well in these neighborhoods.  What is the root cause of this epidemic?

Trauma in the Classroom

# 2

# ROOT CAUSE

"IF YOU CAN SEEK THE CAUSE…

**YOU CAN CHANGE** THE BEHAVIOR."

-JIM SPORLEDER[3]

## --COMMON THREAD--

Behavior is the ultimate form of communication and it became my mission to find out what these kids were trying to say. Careful investigation revealed that each of these students with extreme and severe behavior was attempting to cope with overwhelming stress or trauma in their personal lives. I discovered histories of multiple foster placements (as many as 56 in 6 years), severe domestic violence between parents, homelessness, fear of homelessness, transiency and attendance at as many as 6 schools in one year, victims of physical abuse, neglect, and sexual abuse. I learned that one of our first graders was put into protective custody due to his family's illegal activity and another first grader was forced into her family's business: a prostitution ring. These are just a few examples.

With one exception of actual mental illness, each of these students demonstrating this high level of severe behavior was experiencing extraordinary adversity at home. Not all of the trauma was related to abuse. One boy was playing with matches in the coat closet. He was not abused, but still traumatized when his curiosity caused their family to lose their home in a fire. The trauma was exacerbated when his father died of cancer shortly thereafter. Another young student had two military parents on simultaneous deployment. Though not abuse, this lifestyle proved to be confusing and traumatic for him. Yet another student was living with the stress of having a single mom who was going through chemo-therapy, with no extended family support available. Although not the same stress factor for each student, there was a common-thread: each student was living with at least one source of intense adversity.

I could go on. I could talk about the kindergartener who could not stop running and screaming; he watched his dad shoot his mom. The shot was meant for him, but his mom jumped in the way to provide him protection. I could mention the fifth grader who refused to stay in class and would have violent outbursts without warning, and how he had been in foster care for years waiting to be adopted. I could talk about the kindergartner who would scream, cry and throw things, and the fact that he missed two weeks of school when his mom's boyfriend tried to scrub the marker off his skin. He scrubbed so hard the skin came off too (which just exposed a history of more physical abuse). I could talk about the kindergartner who pushed, poked, bit, spit, and threw objects at others, and I could mention how he watched his dad stab his mom. There was another kindergartener attempting to climb the fence and leave day after day. She was constantly in "flight mode." When I asked her where she was trying to go, she replied with determination, "I need to get to my dad in jail."

## --THE SHORT LIST--

The fact is, just when I think I have heard it all, I hear something new. These situations should be anomalies, but they are not. This is only the short list, I could continue, but most people don't want to know this is going on our schools. They don't want to know that kids are dealing with trauma every day, and they don't want to know these kids with trauma in their lives are disrupting our classrooms so profusely. They want to think these are isolated incidents with rare occurrence. Nobody wants to know that these incidents happen often on many of our campuses. After all, *ignorance is bliss.*

Dr. Nadine Burke Harris addresses this as part of a societal issue. "At first I thought that we marginalized the issue because it doesn't apply to us. That's an issue for *those* kids in *those* neighborhoods. Which is weird, because the data doesn't bear that out... I am beginning to think that maybe I had it completely backwards... I am beginning to believe that we marginalize this issue because *it does apply to us.* Maybe it's easier to see in other zip codes because we don't want to look at it."[4]

It is time to look at it. In my district, we do have schools in *those zip codes*, and those kids are definitely in distress. But we also have those kids and those schools in *our zip codes.* They live across the street, next door, and sometimes, under our rooftops. Harris goes on to say, "The single most important thing that we need today is the courage to look this problem in the face and say, this is real and this is all of us."[5]

### --ROOT CAUSE—

When we discover the root cause of an epidemic, it is our responsibility to do something about it. When we know there is a common thread, we can begin to look for a solution. As a community, we would be furious if doctors discovered a root cause of a health crisis, but then did not look for a cure. We would be livid if prevention was not attempted. We should expect no less than a reasonable solution for our kids in our classrooms who are in crisis. It is time for educators to also stand up with "courage to look this problem in the face and say, this is real and this is all of us."

We need to take a stand.

We need to do it now.

## --FROM THE EXPERTS—

"Sadly, childhood trauma is still the 'elephant in the room.' Unrecognized or unacknowledged and unresolved, it obstructs education efforts and destroys lives."

-Daun Kauffman[6]

"[Childhood trauma is] the single greatest unaddressed public health issue."

-Dr. Vincent Felitti[7]

# Trauma in the Classroom

# 3

# THE TRUTH ABOUT TRAUMA

"REMEMBER: EVERYONE IN THE CLASSROOM HAS A STORY THAT LEADS TO MISBEHAVIOR OR DEFIANCE.

NINE TIMES OUT OF TEN,

**THE STORY** BEHIND THE MISBEHAVIOR WON'T MAKE YOU ANGRY.

IT **WILL BREAK YOUR HEART.**"

— ANNETTE BREAUX[8]

## --THE TRUTH OF THE MATTER--

The severity of trauma these kids experience feeds the belief that trauma in childhood is isolated. After all, most children do not see their parent stabbed or shot. Most kids do not have their skin removed by scrubbing. Most kids don't have parents in jail. Most kids do not wind up in foster care, and those who do usually do not have 56 placements. However, the truth about trauma is this: ***most people experience trauma in childhood.***

## --THE ACEs STUDY--

Kaiser Permanente partnered with the Centers for Disease Control in the 1990s to embark on the first Adverse Childhood Experiences (ACEs) study. The focus of the study was to determine the relationship between these ACEs and health across a life time. The ACEs were divided into categories determined to cause toxic stress during childhood. These categories included: emotional, physical or sexual abuse, emotional or physical neglect, and household dysfunction such as domestic violence against mother, substance abuse within the home, household mental illness, parental separation or divorce, and household member imprisoned. A questionnaire was given to adults and used to determine prevalence of ACEs among respondents. Those results were compared with health outcomes. There was a direct correlation between negative health outcomes and number of ACEs, but more startling was the discovery that over 67% of respondents had at least one of these adverse childhood experiences.[9]

When **two-thirds** of kids experience something, *it is not isolated.*

## --MORE RESEARCH--

That study, published in 1998, was the first of many. Since then, researchers have looked at other stress factors; stress factors that cause, or contribute to trauma. These include, but are not limited to: chronic medical problems for anyone in the home, unmet personal needs, mother with unmanaged post-partum depression, poverty, lack of stimulating environment, racial [or other] discrimination, bullying, very few rules and boundaries, rigid parent(s), domestic fighting or violence, multiple siblings, poor nutrition, death in the family, lack of praise and encouragement, frequent moves, absent parent, overwhelmed parent, exposure to violence in home, community, on T.V. or in video games, blended families, being over scheduled, and feeling pressured from others.[10]

I did my own teacher survey. I asked teachers to generate a list of stress-factors specific to our community. These were elementary school teachers. In addition to the expert lists, they listed circumstances they knew their students (past or present) had experienced. This is their list:

| | |
|---|---|
| parent selling drugs | parental gang activity |
| chronic illness of sibling | homelessness |
| caring for parent | over-exposed to sex |
| parent deported | parent deployed |
| caring for younger siblings | prostitution |
| multiple-family households | hungry |
| unable to keep utilities running | parents work nights |
| going to work with parents | transiency |
| multiple partners (parent) | new-to-country |
| parents caring for extended family | abandonment |

parent does not speak English (and in some instances, student only speaks English)

Many of these factors are just part of life as we have come to know it; yet if all children are going to be exposed to stressors at some level, why does their response vary so widely? The fact is, not all children experiencing adversity become traumatized.

Heather T. Forbes is a Licensed Clinical Social Worker, owner of Beyond Consequences Institute, and a pioneer on the topic of trauma-informed solutions for parents, schools and mental health professionals. In her book, *Help for Billy*, she explains it this way:

> These specific events, however, do not guarantee that the child will be traumatized simply because of the event itself. It is the perception and the emotional interpretation of the event that classifies it as trauma or not. It is about the feeling of being safe or not and it is ***always determined by the child's perspective-*** not reality… Obviously, every child is going to experience some degree of trauma. ***Whether or not the trauma is going to have a lasting effect on the child depends on how well the fundamental needs of physical safety, emotional connection, and predictability are met for the child.*** When children are given environments of support, love, and

attention, and when needs are met, the impact of traumatic experiences is minimized, and in many cases, avoided.[11] *(Emphasis added.)*

Essentially, children who are not traumatized by adversity have in place the right kind of support, feel attached and connected, get enough attention and consistently have their needs met. They believe that they will be safe and secure in spite of the traumatic experience(s). Kids who do not have this level of security experience trauma over and over again. They are not learning that their needs will continually be met in the face of adversity because personal history has shown them otherwise.

Adversity is a part of life, it is certainly a part of childhood. However, when children do not feel supported, safe and secure it becomes a much greater issue.

## --FROM THE EXPERTS--

"The ACEs study is replicated and confirmed over and over again around the world. This defines the human condition."

-Dr. Chris Blodgett [12]

"The combination of the ACE study and all of the other similar research, plus the biological research which shows the mechanisms whereby early, overwhelming stress causes changes in the brain, in the hormonal systems, in stress reactivity, in the genome and the way genes are expressed. All of this creates a very compelling case."

-David Corwin, MD [13]

Children's exposure to family violence is a widespread problem... Studies estimate that between 3.3 million and 10 million children in the U.S. witness violence in their own homes each year.

– Massachusetts Advocates for Children [14]

Trauma in the Classroom

# 4

# TRAUMA AND LEARNING

"THE **STRESS** RESPONSE **MAKES LEARNING DIFFICULT**... THINK ABOUT IT THIS WAY: WOULD YOU BE ABLE TO MEMORIZE THE TIMES TABLES WHEN YOU WERE BEING CHASED BY A BEAR?"

—LEAH LEVEY[15]

## --DISRUPTED DEVELOPMENT--

Although the initial ACEs study focused on the effects of adversity on health outcomes, new research looks specifically at the impact of trauma on learning. As it turns out, trauma interferes with typical development and *actually causes physiological changes that drastically decrease the stressed student's ability to learn.* Extensive study of human biology exposes a harmful link between ongoing toxic stress and problems with perception, memory, organization, planning, processing, natural curiosity, interpreting information, interacting with others and responding to the environment.

Leading experts on child development at Harvard report, "Extensive research on the biology of stress now shows that healthy development can be derailed by excessive or prolonged activation of stress... with damaging effects on learning, [and] behavior..." [16]

In his book *Brain Rules*, Developmental Microbiologist, John Medina (2014) wrote:

If the stress is too severe or too prolonged... [it] begins to harm learning. Stressed people don't do math very well. They don't process language very efficiently. They have poorer memories, both short and long forms. Stressed people do not generalize or adapt old pieces of information to new scenarios as well as non-stressed individuals. They can't concentrate. In almost every way it can be tested, chronic stress hurts our ability to learn. [Additionally,] stress hormones can do some truly nasty things to your brain... Quite literally, severe stress can cause brain damage in the very tissues most likely to help you succeed in life.[17]

## --EARLY ADVERSITY AND THE BRAIN--

Healthy childhood development is essential for the learning process. Early childhood developmental theorists such as Jean Piaget, John Bowbly and B.F. Skinner describe stages of development where children learn to explore their environment in safety; they learn to trust adults and seek help from them; they are able to organize their experiences and discern circumstances that are safe vs. circumstances that are threatening. When outcomes are stable and reliable, they learn cause and effect and how to make predictions. When early childhood development is disrupted, the opposite occurs.

Why does pervasive stress interfere with typical development? Early adversity affects areas such as the pleasure and reward center of the brain, it inhibits the area of the brain responsible for impulse control and executive function and contributes to an over-active fear-response center.[18]

Why does this matter? Children with over-active fear-response centers are hypervigilant. They focus on environmental stimuli rather than on building relationships or academic content. They are over-attuned to irregularities and inconsistencies in their surroundings, which trigger the stress-response system (fight, flight or freeze) and cause inappropriate behavioral responses that are disproportionate to the situation. When the stress-response system is triggered over and over again throughout the child's developmental years, it is difficult for them to perceive any environment as safe. When children perceive their environment as unsafe, they lose their instinctive curiosity. Nurtured curiosity propels children forward in school. Stifled curiosity stifles learning.

In *Beyond Consequences, Logic and Control*, Forbes and Post describe it this way:

Traditionally, we have failed to realize that limited learning will happen if the emotional needs of the child are not met first. The hierarchy of learning… has not traditionally been acknowledged. A child … cannot learn when he is living at the edge of survival- at the edge of his breaking point. Trauma alters to what the brain pays attention, so all [of the child's] resources are dedicated to safety rather than academic achievement. [19]

Additionally, when the development of the pleasure and reward center of the brain is disrupted, children do not understand consequences, or delayed gratification. Their life experience has been largely inconsistent and unpredictable. These inconsistencies leave children without the ability to observe cause and effect patterns that are necessary to both understand consequences and delay gratification. In her book, *Distressed or Deliberately Defiant?*, Dr. Judith A. Howard explains:

[When] the parent cues are confusing… …emotional self-regulation may not develop well and the capacity for successful socialization and the development of inner resilience may be significantly impaired. In addition, the child must live with their perplexing situation of having the same person representing both the source of their protection and the source of their distress.[20]

Without predictable patterns of safe and supportive adult behavior, developing children cannot develop the ability to make predictions or begin to understand the relationship between cause and effect.

Impulse control, executive function and collaboration are also essential to learning. In her book, *Trauma-Sensitive Schools; Learning Communities Transforming Children's Lives, K-5*, Susan E. Craig describes it this way, "Deficits in executive skills make organizing materials and meeting deadlines difficult, while a disproportionately high level of problematic peer relationships limits their capacity for collaborative small-group work."[21]

Quite literally, when children are living in circumstances that do not offer stability, support and safety, their ability to perceive, process and learn is significantly, adversely altered.

## --ACCOUNTABILITY--

Federal and state laws hold teachers and administrators accountable for failing students. Yet, the needs of these students are being overlooked. They will continue to fail until the core of the problem is addressed. As reported by Jane Ellen Stevens in Aces Too High News, the *Journal of Child Abuse and Neglect* published study in 2011 exposing the relationship between ACEs and learning problems. "Of the kids with zero ACEs, 97% had no learning problems. But half the kids with an ACE score of 4 or higher had learning problems."[22] In fact, study after study demonstrates that people do not learn effectively when they are experiencing high doses of stress or trauma. The problem for these students is quite simple: *when a student is exposed to prolonged stress outside of school, he is not equipped to learn while he is at school.*

We will not achieve greater gains through more academic instruction. Response to Intervention (RTI) began as an effort to target academic deficits of students who are not responding to traditional classroom instruction, but are not receiving special education services. Yet, according to a 2015 U.S. Department of Education study, "Students on RTI fell further behind grade level instead of catching up."[23] There are many speculations as to why this is happening, but we must look at trauma as a potential cause. If we pair the results of this study, with the results published in the *Journal of Child Abuse and Neglect*, 50% of our students with ACE scores of 4 or more have learning problems, indicating that many of the students receiving RTI for academic deficits are also victims of childhood adversity.

Perhaps RTI is not working because we are using the wrong intervention! Providing targeted academic instruction in academic deficit areas will not work with these students because their deficits are deeper than academic skill sets. They are not ***skill deficient***, they are ***need deficient***. Federal subsidies allow kids to be fed at school. Community donations put shoes on their feet and jackets on their backs. There is no subsidy available to help students who are victims of emotional trauma.

In fact, research tells us that until student needs are met, we cannot expect academic interventions to yield the kind of results we are looking for. Still, teachers are expected to teach bell-to-bell, teach more, and provide more academic interventions. After-school tutoring, intercession tutoring, lunch tutoring, more homework, more classwork; these are the solutions being offered and pushed. Yet, nothing is in place to sufficiently address the needs of these kids.

The legislation ensures that academic institutions are taking steps to reduce the achievement gap for other subgroups, but the needs of these students in this unidentified subgroup continue to go unaddressed. In order for administrators to get closer to actually ensuring that every student succeeds, the root cause of this disruption to learning must be acknowledged and interventions must appropriately match the deficit.

## --FROM THE EXPERTS--

Trauma contributes to lower grade point averages, absenteeism, dropping-out, suspensions and expulsions, and decreased reading ability.

– The National Child Traumatic Stress Network[24]

"The greatest inhibitor of long-term memory formation is the opposite of relaxed states- stress. Not just some annoying side effect of our modern world, stress can affect learning and memory by producing devastating changes in your body… producing dramatic changes in your brain…"

– Advanced Learning Institute[25]

"The science is clear: overly stressed students struggle to maintain self-control, their long and short-term memory is impacted, they struggle with emotional control, focus, the ability to initiate a task, planning, organizing and time awareness. They lack flexibility, moral judgement and logical and sequential thinking. They lack interpersonal skills."[26]

-Heather T. Forbes

"Traumatized children have lower scores on standardized tests, higher referrals to special education, higher dropout rates, and are more likely than peers to engage in delinquent behavior."

-Susan E. Craig[27]

Trauma in the Classroom

# 5

## TRAUMA AND BEHAVIOR

"IF SOMETHING DOESN'T CHANGE THE COURSE OF THEIR LIVES, THE PRIVATE ISSUE OF **RAISING SUCH CHILDREN** SOON **WILL BECOME A** VERY **PUBLIC PROBLEM**."

–DR. JOHN MEDINA[28]

## --EVOLUTION OF STUDENT BEHAVIOR--

Student behavior has always had a direct effect on teaching and learning in the classroom. In *The First Days of School*, Harry Wong stated, "Education is not teaching people things they don't currently know. Education is teaching people behaviors they don't currently practice"[29] The problem is found in the nature and evolution of student behavior. Techniques commonly relied upon to influence student behavior are not proving effective for our students with the most disruptive, most severe behavior.

## --WHAT ARE TEACHERS SAYING?--

According to a random sample survey of 725 secondary-level teachers, conducted by Public Agenda and supported by Common Good, 97% of teachers believe that appropriate behavior is required in order for students to succeed; 93% believe that students need to learn to follow the rules in order to be contributing members of society.[30] The same survey indicated that 85% of teachers feel the learning of other students is impacted greatly by persistent behavior problems, while 77% of these teachers indicate that the amount of time spent handling the disruptions impacts their effectiveness as instructors.

One-third of teachers surveyed have either considered a career change or know someone who has changed professions **strictly due to student behavior**. Eighty-five percent of those surveyed believe new teachers are not equipped to deal with the current behavior trends.[31]

This survey is eleven-years old, but the behavior problems still persist. In fact, a separate survey conducted by Scholastic in partnership with the Bill and Melinda Gates Foundation finds that "the increased level of behavior problems has been seen across grade levels… 68% of elementary teachers surveyed indicate that behavior problems are on the rise…More than half of teachers wish they could spend less time disciplining students."[32]

### *That is the problem.*

Teachers have always been called upon to manage student behavior, but these behaviors are on the rise. The nature and severity of individual student behavior is such that it is not only impacting the individual student's learning, but also the learning of others. Not only is the behavior itself disruptive, but the level of human resources required to maintain students with these behaviors is disproportionate. The increased level of personnel support required also decreases the availability of those resources for the remainder of the student body. Medina warned that if we did not address this "the private issue of raising such children soon will become a very public problem."[33] I am a witness that in our schools, *it already is.*

## --COPING MECHANISMS--

Science clearly demonstrates that toxic levels of stress interfere with learning by literally changing the way the brain works; but it also demonstrates that toxic stress interferes with behavioral control for the same reason. The problem for these children lies within their over-used stress-response system.

The stress-response system is necessary for survival. It is how our ancestors survived. It is how our bodies are programmed to get out of precarious, dangerous situations. It is often described as the fight, flight or freeze response. This system is designed to react quickly when needed, but is also designed to lie in a protective state of vigilance when we perceive a situation or environment as a potential threat. When the stress-response system of a developing child is over-activated, the child becomes naturally hypervigilant due to the perception that all situations and environments are in fact, potential threats. When you have a hypervigilant student who is over-attuned to environmental cues, you also have a student who can be quickly overcome by the stress-response to fight, flee or freeze.

The behavior is confusing for the majority because we view the environment as safe. Teachers and even other students usually cannot identify a specific trigger for the behavior simply because they do not view the environment with the same level of caution as the over-stressed child. Additionally, the behavior display is disproportionate to the event, and often determined to be irrational by onlookers.

Trauma and Learning Policy Initiative (TLPI), a collaboration of Massachusetts Advocates for Children and Harvard Law School reports:

> For many children who have experienced traumatic events, the school setting can feel like a battleground in which their assumptions of the world as a dangerous place sabotage their ability to remain calm and regulate their behavior in the classroom. Unfortunately, *many of these children develop behavioral coping mechanisms in an effort to feel safe and in control,* yet these behaviors can frustrate educators and evoke exasperated reprisals, reactions

that both strengthen the child's expectations of confrontation and danger and reinforce a negative self-image.[34] *(Emphasis added.)*

Forbes and Post state:

> [We see] an overly stressed out child who has difficulty interacting in relationships, who struggles to behave in a loving way, who quite often cannot think clearly, and who swings back and forth in his emotional states due to an underdeveloped regulatory system. While perceived by most professionals as dangerous, a child of trauma is essentially a scared child- a stressed child living out of a primal, survival mode in order to maintain his existence.[35]

### --LEARNING INTERFERES WITH BEHAVIOR--

These children, *these students,* often present with behaviors that are inconsistent with learning. In fact, the question posed by educators is quite often: "does the behavior interfere with the learning of the student?" When in fact, as science has uncovered, it is learning that is interfering with the behavior. When a child is in a constant state of distress, it is impossible to learn behavior expectations through observation alone, and those fight, flight or freeze behaviors continue to be activated over and over again. In the classroom, the behavior of these overly-stressed students looks like: kicking, hitting, biting, spitting, elopement, cursing, verbal threats, crying, tantrums, refusing to talk, refusing to work, becoming immobile, rocking, trying to hide, etc.[36] It can also include symptoms of anxiety, impulsivity, forgetfulness, pervasive tardies, chronic absenteeism, risk taking, defiance, and an inability to sit or be still. Not all behaviors stand out. Some kids grow detached and separate themselves from classroom events. They may sleep in class, refuse to participate, and disengage from peers and adults. As a behavior interventionist, I respond to the most severe of these behaviors. ***Classroom teachers respond to them all.***

Why is learning interfering with behavior? Albert Bandura, psychologist and father of Social Learning Theory taught us that, "Learning would be exceedingly laborious, not to mention hazardous, if people had to rely solely on the effects of their own actions to inform them what to do." [37] The problem for children dealing with pervasive stress is two-fold. Not only are they hypervigilant and living on the edge of fear in order to survive, but they also do not have that reliable, predictable model that helps them organize their experience. They are living in circumstances where they truly are relying "solely on the effects of their own actions to inform them what to do."

## --FROM THE EXPERTS--

"Children with toxic stress live much of their lives in fight, flight or fright (freeze) mode. They respond to the world as a place of constant danger. With their brains overloaded with stress hormones and unable to function appropriately, they can't focus on learning. They fall behind in school or fail to develop healthy relationships with peers or create problems with teachers and principals because they are unable to trust adults. Some kids do all three."

– Jane Ellen Stevens[38]

"Some of these children may express emotions without restraint and seem impulsive, under-controlled, unable to reflect, edgy, oversensitive, or aggressive."

– Massachusetts Advocates for Children[39]

"We have to take care of the emotional side as well as the academic side of teaching to create an environment where children are able to learn."

-Tammy Worth[40]

"Be aware of both the children who act out AND the quiet children who don't appear to have behavioral problems. These students often 'fly beneath the radar' and do not get help. They may have symptoms of avoidance and depression that are just as serious as those of the acting out student."

–The National Child Traumatic Stress Network[41]

# 6

# WHAT THIS MEANS FOR TEACHERS

## "TRAUMA

IS NOT JUST A MENTAL HEALTH PROBLEM.
IT IS AN EDUCATIONAL PROBLEM THAT, LEFT
UNADDRESSED,

**DERAILS** THE **ACADEMIC ACHIEVEMENT**

OF THOUSANDS OF CHILDREN."

-SUSAN E. CRAIG[42]

## --PREPARATION--

The problem so often is that teachers are not prepared to handle behaviors of students who are experiencing toxic stress. I did a survey with teachers at one of my elementary schools. While almost every teacher stated that they have between 1-5 children with pervasive, disruptive behaviors each school year, 69% of those surveyed said they do not feel equipped to handle these behavior problems; just 4% said they do. (The rest declined to respond.) I find this alarming. When we leave teachers ill-equipped to handle their students, how can we expect teachers or students to be successful?

## --DISCIPLINE PRACTICES--

Current discipline practices include: behavior citations, detention, conferences with the student, conferences with the parent, and progressive suspensions which may lead to expulsion. Current behavior management strategies include: behavior contracts, behavior plans, reward systems. Reactive strategies for disruptions include: ignoring the behavior while it is occurring, removing the rest of the students when safety is in jeopardy, calling additional adult supports for back-up, calling parents for back-up, and even, at times, calling school police.

The disruptive student is habitually removed from the classroom in order to maintain the learning environment for the rest of the students. This can lead to a student falling behind grade level expectations simply due to lack of exposure to the curriculum. When students are already receiving special education services, it also contributes to a loss of services required by the student's Individualized Education Plan (IEP). This leaves teachers feeling a greater sense of urgency when it comes to meeting the instructional needs of these children. This sense of urgency can lead to increased demands when the student is in the room, which in turn, leads to an increase in behavior problems.

This cycle also increases the sense of urgency teachers feel for the other students in the class. They begin to feel guilty for the time they spend responding to behaviors and the overall reduction in instruction. Their urgency and guilt then influences their response to disruptive students- it is a nasty cycle without a clear end in sight. The cycle exists because our teachers are uninformed of the effects of trauma and ill-equipped to respond to students in distress.

Abraham Maslow, psychologist, said, "I suppose it is tempting, if the only tool you have is a hammer, to treat everything as if it were a nail."[43] This is the current problem for educators. We have given them a tool, but it is not the right one for this issue.

Dr. Judith A. Howard says, "What we commonly depend on to manage student behavior may **actually make things worse for these students.** "[44] Heather T. Forbes, LCSW wrote, "The solutions that are traditionally in place for children with challenging, difficult and even severe behaviors are not working. They are failing our children in the classroom. Or more importantly, we are failing our children in the classroom" [45]

If leading experts continue to warn that traditional methods do not work, why do educational policies and systems remain the same? *Why aren't we giving teachers a different tool?*

## --FAILING TRADITIONS--

We **ARE** failing our children in the classroom. We aren't just failing those with evidence of trauma and disrupted childhood development; we are failing all of the other students who **ARE** ready to learn, because we aren't changing the way we teach and the way we respond to children in distress. It is foolish to think the impact is isolated. We are also failing our teachers, because we aren't taking steps to inform them of this science fast enough.

We continue to leave them year after year, using methods of classroom management that do not help these kids. We continue to demand increased rigor, increased academic interventions, increased time in the classroom in an attempt to increase achievement, but we are overlooking a simple fact: these kids are not ready to learn. ***Their foundational needs of safety, security, and basic self-regulation are missing.*** We leave our teachers feeling deflated and burned-out with *increased demands* and *decreased power* and ability to teach. The reality is, we should be moving mountains to get this information in their hands. We need to give them back the hope they have lost through failed experiences. By doing so, we will be giving hope to these children, hope for the future.

## --FROM THE EXPERTS--

"Teaching is mainly concerned with the cognitive domain. Yet limiting teaching to that one domain does not prepare us for the classroom, especially when working with students with disruptive behavior."

Sharon Longert[46]

"Too often we respond negatively to a child who is seeking attention or whose behavior is confusing or oppositional, when the child may be desperately in need of connection to peers and adults. We too easily discipline students for an inappropriate response to an adult, labeling it disrespect, rather than recognizing it as the student's halting or awkward effort to relate."

-Massachusetts Advocates for Children [47]

"The way our educational system is set up is to really support the teacher, to be the best teacher possible with the best instructional materials or technology. If we focus entirely on that, and there's trauma in the classroom and the teacher is not prepared to deal with that barrier or is not aware of the barrier, it doesn't matter how good of a teacher she or he is or what type of instructional material they have… That's why we have a big miss academically."

-Pia Escudero[48]

Trauma in the Classroom

# 7

## Healing: One Child at a Time

"To the world you may be one person;

but to one person,

**you may be the world.**"

–Dr. Seuss[49]

## --MRS. RYAN AND JAYLA--

Mrs. Ryan is a first-grade teacher in a small, Southern California school district. She has thirty-two first-grade students, four exhibit chronic, disruptive behaviors. One student, we'll call her Jayla, joined the class in October. In November, she began to engage in minor disruptions, such as refusing to work and refusing to follow directions. Mrs. Ryan uses a system of positive reinforcement in the classroom, but Jayla's behavior not only did not improve, but continued to escalate.

## --THE HULK--

Jayla's behavior intensified from refusing to follow directions to crying, then screaming, and then by the end of January, she was swiping materials off of desks, throwing pencils, markers, books, and even chairs. At times, Mrs. Ryan's other students were required to go outside and wait for Jayla to calm down. The students became fearful of Jayla and even referred to her as "The Hulk." Jayla's behavior did not follow a predictable pattern. She just seemed to lose control without warning.

### --"My Brain's Going Crazy!"--

One day Jayla began throwing things- including chairs. She was throwing anything she could touch, and tearing things off walls so she could keep throwing more. Mrs. Ryan got the rest of the students out of the room to safety, called for adult assistance, and then went back to help Jayla. From the doorway, Mrs. Ryan shouted, "**Jayla**, come here and give me a hug!" Jayla was stunned to silence and stillness, and quickly obliged. With arms wrapped around Mrs. Ryan, Jayla cried and cried. When she started to settle, Mrs. Ryan asked, "Jayla, what's going on?" Her tone was not accusatory, but patient, genuine and unconditional. She wanted to know. Jayla answered, "I don't know. Sometimes my brain feels like it is going crazy and I don't know how to make it stop."

Mrs. Ryan stood there with Jayla until Jayla was calm and back in control. Without prompting, Jayla looked at the results of her behavior and apologized for making such a mess and volunteered to clean it up. Jayla took responsibility for her behavior, cleaned up the mess and was then able to remain calm and safe.

## --THE POWER OF A HUG--

The next day, Mrs. Ryan met Jayla at the door and told her that if she felt like her brain was starting to go crazy again, she needed to come get a hug right away- before she had a chance to lose control. Jayla wanted a LOT of hugs that morning. That day wasn't perfect. She had another moment when her "brain went crazy." As a result, she had to go home, but before she left, Mrs. Ryan told her she loved her and loved having her in her class and could not wait for her to come back. She did not condemn the behavior.

On the third day, Jayla was reminded to seek hugs, and she did seek hugs. So many in fact, that Mrs. Ryan thought she might be trying to manipulate her circumstances. But, Mrs. Ryan always accommodated; that was their deal, and she knew part of this intervention process was establishing herself as a trustworthy adult. Jayla was able to keep calm the entire day. She didn't do the same independent work the other kids were doing, but Mrs. Ryan wanted her to be successful being calm. She wanted Jayla to practice being calm, and practice signaling her when she felt stressed, so she didn't require the work.

## --EXPECTATIONS--

However, on the fourth day, Mrs. Ryan put the same morning work on Jayla's desk that she did on all the other 31 desks. When Jayla came in, before she had the opportunity to get upset, Mrs. Ryan looked her in the eyes and tenderly, yet firmly said, "Jayla, when you are finished with your math, you may use my iPad." Jayla did her math without complaint. When it was time to give up the iPad, Jayla did so, also without complaint. Within four-days' time, Mrs. Ryan was able to move Jayla safely back to a place where she was ready to learn.

It sounds like a fairy tale, but it is not. This is an actual account of an actual teacher in actual first grade class with 32 students. Mrs. Ryan changed her approach to Jayla because she recognized that Jayla was in distress. She recognized that traditional methods of behavior management were escalating the behaviors, not reducing them, and she found research that supported her experience and gave her new ideas.

I followed Jayla's story closely. There is a lot of research that tells us what we can do to help these kids, but it's not just about what the research says, it's about application of the research on individuals. That is what this is about: helping individuals, one child at a time.

## --STOP AND BREATHE--

It would be a lie to say Jayla was in control of every moment from there on. In fact, Jayla would often get antsy and agitated. But, Mrs. Ryan had a few other strategies. She taught the whole class how to recognize anxious feelings and then taught them to "stop and breathe" when they start to feel uneasy. She taught them to help each other recognize body language that indicates they are getting frustrated, and to help each other remember to "stop and breathe." Several times a day kids shout, "stop and breathe- it's okay!" Jayla responds to her friends when they try to help her. A few kids went beyond that and would ask Jayla if she needed a hug. Jayla gladly accepted hugs from any of her peers who offered them. She used these hugs to regroup so she could rejoin the class emotionally. Mrs. Ryan did not have to help Jayla alone; she had 31 first graders helping as well.

## --INTERNAL BATTLE--

Mrs. Ryan created a safe and secure classroom environment for Jayla, and for the other students, but it took effort. Mrs. Ryan reported that it was really difficult because the seasoned part of her wanted Jayla to just behave as expected. The rational brain told her that she was a teacher and Jayla was a child; her authority should have been enough to cause Jayla to change her behavior. Mrs. Ryan admitted that the authoritative side of her really struggled with this new, non-traditional approach; the devil on her shoulder was hard at work. But, in her heart, she knew it was what Jayla needed. She knew Jayla was not choosing her behavior. She knew Jayla struggled to control her own thoughts, emotions and actions and needed help. She saw how quickly Jayla responded to the changed response and knew it was working.

She believed in the idea that one person really can make a difference. She was that person for Jayla.

Trauma in the Classroom

# 8

# THE GOAL OF PUBLIC EDUCATION

"**THE FUTURE OF** ANY **SOCIETY DEPENDS ON** ITS ABILITY TO FOSTER HEALTHY DEVELOPMENT OF **THE NEXT GENERATION**. EXTENSIVE RESEARCH ON THE BIOLOGY OF STRESS NOW SHOWS THAT HEALTHY DEVELOPMENT CAN BE DERAILED BY EXCESSIVE OR PROLONGED ACTIVATION OF STRESS… WITH DAMAGING EFFECTS ON LEARNING, [AND] BEHAVIOR…"
-HARVARD UNIVERSITY, CENTER ON THE DEVELOPING CHILD [50]

## --FULFILLING THEIR POTENTIAL--

When school-board members were asked to rank their goals for public education, the number one response was to "help students fulfill their potential." Second was to, "Prepare students for [a] satisfying and productive life."[51] The fact is, *trauma directly interferes with the primary goals of the public school system*. Or maybe it is not the trauma that is interfering with the mission, but rather our response to trauma that is getting in the way.

How is that so? Traditionally, in order to both help students fulfill their potential and prepare them to live satisfying and productive lives, the education system looks for ways to increase rigor. Districts adopt intervention approaches which target primarily reading and math. Monies are pumped into programs designed to increase academic abilities such as after-school tutoring, intercession tutoring, Saturday school, etc. These traditional methods simply are not a satisfactory way to help students of trauma fulfill their potential, or live satisfying and productive lives. In fact, research is now showing us that these increased academic pressures can contribute to the stress of an already stressed-out child.

## --Short-term Results--

Traditionally, when student behavior is chronic, severe, dangerous or disruptive, schools respond with punitive disciplinary tactics. Students spend time "on the wall," time in the principal's office, and time in detention. They are removed from campus temporarily via suspension, or permanently via expulsion. Many of these children will ultimately qualify for special education services as a student with an emotional disability. These traditions are counter-productive. They keep kids out of the classroom, off our campuses, and away from their peers. Although an immediate solution for serious behavior, these responses only yield short-term results. Unfortunately, these short-term results actually interfere with long-term progress and helping students reach their potential.

As a system, we need to step back and ask if we believe education is about helping **ALL** kids fulfill their potential. If this is not the mission, then we are free to go on with our traditional (yet failing) practices. If it is, then we **MUST** look at the needs of our kids in distress. We cannot ignore the science. It is perfectly clear. In order to reach this group of kids, we have to satisfy their emotional needs. We need to establish school environments that are predictable, emotionally safe, stable, forgiving, tolerant, and provide alternate, supportive settings for kids in crisis. In order to help them fulfill their potential, we need to build their foundation on Maslow's hierarchy by satisfying not only their physical needs, but their emotional needs, including the ability to self-manage their emotions. We need to help our kids who come to school unprepared to learn, get ready to learn. If we are going to also help our kids who DO come to school ready to learn, then we need to provide them an environment where disruptions are limited, so they too, are able to fulfill their potential.

## --FROM THE EXPERTS--

"Trauma is not just a mental health problem. It is an educational problem that, left unaddressed, derails the academic achievement of thousands of children."

-Susan E. Craig[52]

"Untreated trauma is so costly to our society. These are the kids who drop out of school, end up in the juvenile justice system, [are victims of] early death and [display] very maladapted behaviors that cost us. But the fact [is] that we can see children bounce back [when they] learn skills and get some support."

-Pia Escuardo[53]

Trauma in the Classroom

# 9

# TRIAGE IN THE CLASSROOM

YOU HAVE TO **TAKE CARE** OF THE

URGENT

IN ORDER TO GET TO THE

IMPORTANT.

– DR. CHRIS BLODGETT[54]

## --A SENSE OF URGENCY--

If I am having a heart attack, and the doctors in the E.R. discover that I have a urinary tract infection (UTI), I am pretty confident they will not ignore the heart attack and treat the UTI first. Although it is *important* to treat the UTI, it is *urgent* to take care of my heart. If they don't get my heart stabilized, it is not going to matter how much effort they put into treating the UTI. Additionally, if I go into the E.R. and have a UTI, but someone else comes in having a heart attack, I fully expect the E.R. doctors to treat the patient in crisis first. The same philosophy is true for running triage in our classrooms.

We have to treat the *urgent* so we can get to the things that are *important.*

Unfortunately, the measure of their success is often judged by test scores. Teachers feel the pressure of the expectation of their job, and often are not even allowed *time* to run student triage. Instead they are expected to follow the plans, stick to the pacing guides, teach bell-to-bell. They are expected to bridge the gap from where the students are to where they should be: academically; but they aren't allowed to start with emotional needs, regardless of the child's crisis, or readiness to learn.

Teachers are constantly challenged with the pressure of the important, and certainly student achievement is important. The problem is, if we don't allow teachers to take care of the urgent, they will never be able to satisfactorily get to the important.

In our schools, the solution for these kids is traditionally to send them home until their crisis is resolved. Can you imagine that response in the E.R.?

*"Oh, I am sorry ma'am; it looks like you are having a heart attack. Go home and come back when your crisis is over."*

The emergency must be addressed, not ignored, not passed on to the office, and certainly not sent home for the day.

## --From the Experts--

The emotional brain always trumps the logical brain. If the emotional brain is not calm, the logical brain cannot be accessed.

- Erika Ryst[55]

ACEs are the single most important predictor of academic success… The higher the number of ACEs, the lower the literacy rate.

– Chris Blodgett[56]

# 10

# TREATMENT IN THE CLASSROOM

"WHEN LITTLE PEOPLE ARE OVERWHELMED

BY **BIG** EMOTIONS, IT'S OUR **JOB TO**

**SHARE OUR CALM,**

NOT JOIN THEIR CHAOS."

-L.R. KNOST[57]

## --BEDSIDE MANNER--

According to a study by the Associated Press-NORC Center for Public Affairs Research, 59% of Americans view the physician-patient relationship **the most important factor** in choosing and keeping a doctor. Additionally, 80% of Americans rate the amount of <u>time</u> a physician spends with each patient as "extremely," or "very important." In other words, according to patients, the most important quality for a doctor is **bedside manner.**[58]

In a separate survey, T. Bradbury asked adult employees why they leave their jobs. He found that of people who quit their jobs, more than half of them cited their relationship with their boss as the cause. "Bosses who fail to really care will always have high turnover rates. It is impossible to work for someone eight-plus hours a day when they aren't personally involved and don't care about anything other than your production yield."[59]

It is evident that relationships are important to adults. It should be no surprise that the best "treatment" for chronically stressed children is also the relationship. Heather T. Forbes wrote: "Interactive repair, or simply a safe relationship is what it takes. **The most important and most effective 'behavioral technique'** [these students] need in order to move them back within the behavioral boundaries of the classroom **is relationship.** Too much emphasis has been placed on what behavioral techniques should be used or which punishments should be imposed… it is the relationship that is actually the driving force behind the change and helping children to get back on course." [60] *(Emphasis added.)*

Think about Mrs. Ryan and Jayla for a moment. The first thing Mrs. Ryan did was to establish herself as someone Jayla could trust. She did this by remaining calm and non-judgmental when Jayla's behavior was uncontrolled. She did this by establishing an emotional connection with Jayla: remember the hug? Mrs. Ryan immediately became a safety net for Jayla. Jayla knew Mrs. Ryan would help her when she felt like her "brain was going crazy." Within the boundaries of a safe relationship, Jayla was able to begin to develop other skills necessary for emotional competency.

While relationship is essential to move forward, it is not the only required step. Aces Too High News reports, "The good news is that kids' brains are plastic. If they develop a trusted relationship with a caring adult, **if they're taught how to calm themselves, if they spend more time in a resilience-building environment than a traumatic**

**environment, their brains will heal** and they will become happy and eternally curious learning sponges — i.e., their natural state of being"[61] *(Emphasis added.)*

Once that relationship is established, kids need to be taught how to cope, how to self-regulate. Mrs. Ryan took the whole-group approach to this. She taught the whole class to not only "stop and breathe," but also to help each other remember to stop and breathe. She really accomplished three things with this one step. First, she established a simple coping mechanism for Jayla to use (along with getting that hug whenever she needed it). Second, she established a caring community of children who made it their objective to look out for each other. In addition to these factors, Mrs. Ryan also inadvertently created a reminder for herself. She readily acknowledged how difficult it was to change her habits to meet the needs of Jayla. She admitted that the "stop and breathe" cue her first graders adopted so quickly helped her remember to also," stop and breathe." This gets her re-focused on her objective to use the trauma-sensitive approach before she has time to let old habits resurface.

The research and science align without deviation. Study after study demonstrates that healing can occur when children are placed in supportive environments with supportive adults. This environment Mrs. Ryan created in her classroom is a resilience-building environment. Keeping Jayla at school allows her to spend more time working on self-regulation and her coping skills (as well as her academics). This environment began the healing Jayla needed in order to get back on track. Mrs. Ryan did this without additional resources, with thirty-two kids in her room.

## --THE RESPONSE TEAM—

Imagine for a moment, an E.R. movie scene.

Here is the script:

**Nurse 1:** *(panicky, screaming)* OH @!$@!! The patient is crashing! Doctor, Doctor! *(runs to doorway)* **SOMEONE GET A DOCTOR!!!!!** *(turning back to patient)* @!$@!! It's getting worse, **WE NEED MORE DOCTORS!**

**Nurse 2:** *(sounding inconvenienced)* Oh jeez, here we go again. *(rolls eyes)* I don't know why we keep trying to save this patient. This is like the fifth time in 90 minutes. There is no hope, we are just spinning our wheels. This is such a waste of time. *(throws up hands and then begins working on patient)*

*Comforting?*

**NO!**

Chaos, fear and doubt are never comforting.

This is *NOT* the way it plays out in an emergency room. Even when the patient is in crisis, the response team is calm and collected. They take control of the situation in such a way that patient and onlookers feel confident in medical staff abilities. Hospital staff may feel a great sense of urgency, perhaps some level inadequacy, and sometimes, just maybe, a little bit of despair; but the patient and onlookers will never know. The responders *respond,* they **do not *react,*** to the situation. They are in control because they have prepared for an emergency such as this. Even though the crisis varies from one patient to the next, the team responds expertly because they have a plan, they know the plan, and they work the plan.

When responding to children in crisis in the classroom, we must respond the same way. We must not allow ourselves to become part of the chaos, but must calmly take action in order to *relieve* the chaos and eliminate the doubt and fear.

### --DO NO HARM--

Another piece of patient treatment is to remain neutral and objective. Surely, physicians have opinions about patient self-care, or even patient inability or unwillingness to follow doctor's orders; nevertheless, they do not let these opinions interfere with their treatment. They objectively treat the problem without passing judgement. "First, do no harm," applies not only to the physical well-being of the patient, but the emotional and mental well-being of the patient as well. Teachers also need to adopt this philosophy to *first, do no harm*. Erika Ryst, Child and Adolescent Psychiatry issues this charge, "We cannot be the cause of trauma, we have to be the solution."[62]

When a child is in crisis in the classroom, all children in the room need the adult(s) to remain calm and take control of the situation. They need to know there is a plan and the adult(s) are going to work the plan. When the crisis is over, the distressed child needs to have the opportunity to "save face." Imagine how a child must feel, having lost control due to an inability to interpret and harness emotional responses, and imagine how that child must feel knowing her peers just watched it all. The best thing a teacher can do for a child after a crisis is to remain neutral, pass no judgement, and provide an unconditional, genuine relationship and an emotionally safe environment.

## --COMPASSION--

It is also important for educators to exercise compassion. Travis Stephensen, physician and author of *Exploring Edges*, has made it his mission to not only heal physical infirmities, but also heal the spirits of others. Using social media he posts a daily "Awesome thing of the day" segment. One entry reads:

Awesome thing of the day: Meaningful interactions with patients. I had a patient who was really upset today. She was so frustrated with her illness and that no one could do anything about it. Though I was paged three times during our conversation, I stayed with her to listen to her, and feel the full intensity of her sadness with her and to do what I could. At the end I asked if I could give her a hug. She said yes, and broke down in tears as I hugged her. I told her that if I could, I would take the pain for her. And that made me cry because I meant it.

Though it hurts, being a doctor is awesome. And so are hugs.[63]

In this instance, Stephensen could not heal this patient's health; but he could help her find some peace. He gave of his time. He provided some emotional security. He showed genuine concern, and exercised compassion.

It can be difficult to accept and understand the mechanism of the behavior of these students. It requires a mind-shift. When educators shift their attitudes and perspectives of these children, when they stop looking at "what's wrong" with the student and start wondering "what happened"[64] to the child, they are in a better position to give their time, show genuine concern, and exercise compassion.

## --FROM THE EXPERTS--

"A child's nervous system and neurological pathways have plasticity: the ability to change, adapt, acquire, and create new and improved neurological pathways. It is in the relationship and emotional states of fear and overwhelm that the damage happens, so it stands to reason that it is in the relationship and emotional states of safety and love that repair and healing happen…. Profound changes and healing can occur when a child is placed in the right environment; when his needs are met; when the relationships in his life offer acceptance, trust, and understanding; and when given the chance to have positive repetitious experiences in order to override past negative repetitious experiences."

- Heather T. Forbes [65]

"The negative effects of toxic stress can be lessened with the support of caring adults. Appropriate support and intervention can help in returning the stress response system back to its normal baseline."

-Centers for Disease Control [66]

# 11

## PREVENTION

"IT TAKES A VILLAGE TO **RAISE**

**A CHILD.**"

-AFRICAN PROVERB[67]

## --OUNCE OF PREVENTION, A POUND OF CURE--

All good physicians talk about prevention, not just about treatment or cures. Educators must have a similar conversation. Our first responsibility to our community's children is to allow them to live in safety: free from fear. Trauma strips that freedom away from our kids.

While as educators we cannot control circumstances or environments outside of our school, we can definitely control the circumstances and environment within the school. First and foremost, we need to NOT contribute to the existing trauma. If unpredictable adult behavior leads to confusion, hyper-vigilance, and activation of the stress-response system, then **WE MUST BE PREDICTABLE**. We are predictable when we communicate clearly, when our actions are consistent with our words, when expectations are established and enforced, and we respond to events rather than react to them.

Additionally, in order to avoid re-activating previously lived trauma, we need to teach kids how to deal with stress. They struggle at school because their stress-response system has been activated over and over again, and they have never learned how to manage the emotions tied to this reaction. We do not need to have special counseling groups for kids to learn these coping skills. All kids in all classrooms, in all grades will benefit from learning strategies for dealing with stress. If students are taught coping skills as a Tier I strategy from the very first day of school, all students will be more prepared to deal with the stress that occurs when a classmate is in distress. The students living in distress will benefit from repeated practice of these skills when they are calm, so they know how to use them when they begin to feel, well, like their "brain is going crazy."

Mrs. Ryan taught her whole class to "stop and breathe." She reported that this significantly altered the climate of her classroom. The other kids were no longer afraid of Jayla because they had a tool to both manage their own stress and help Jayla manage hers. In fact, the students were able to increase the preventive measures in the class and increase success for everyone. Her students were no longer afraid to interact with Jayla *because they understood* and were given a method to help.

One other key to prevention is **shared adult understanding.** Mrs. Ryan set out to try something different for her students in her class, but she was doing this alone. This caused some conflicts for Jayla. One day,

Jayla got in trouble before school started and before Mrs. Ryan could get to her. She was assigned lunch detention by another adult. Jayla had a difficult time that day. She had her recess taken from her before the school day even started. In her mind, she had already failed and trying no longer served a purpose. Mrs. Ryan had to be extra vigilant just to keep Jayla, and her other students, safe throughout the day.

On another day, school police were on campus. Jayla saw the police and immediately started to shake in reaction. The sight of police obviously triggered a memory and emotion for her. Mrs. Ryan had to stay with Jayla during lunch that day. Jayla sat next to Mrs. Ryan with her hand on Mrs. Ryan's knee- she was petrified. Luckily, Mrs. Ryan had already established herself as that safe adult for Jayla. With Mrs. Ryan by her side, Jayla was able to maintain emotional control, even in her moment of fear.

Although Mrs. Ryan was able to keep Jayla safe on these days, imagine how it would be if all the adults on campus had a shared understanding. Prevention requires knowledge. People cannot do what they do not know, or understand what they have never learned. Prevention requires us to *educate our educators*. Prevention requires them to know about the effects of trauma, and to know how they can be part of the healing.

One question I get frequently is, "How do we know if the behavior is a result of trauma?" The answer: ***We don't always know.*** It is impossible to know every child's back-story. I was supporting a kindergarten student with extraordinarily escalated behaviors. This student would climb on furniture, crawl under furniture, scream and yell, throw things, run from one section of the room to another, hit, kick, pinch, poke, push, bite and pull hair. His behavior was so severe that he required direct adult assistance all day.

After about two months of complete chaos for this student, his grandmother disclosed at least some of his source of toxic stress. This five-year-old had been neglected by one parent (neighbors reported this when he knocked on their door at 10:00 at night, begging for food.) Additionally, his parents were abusive to each other and he had witnessed domestic violence over and over again. One parent served jail-time for the violence, another had a restraining order and no longer had contact with the boy. When this information was disclosed, some of the supporting adults said, "If only I had known that from the beginning, I could have handled things differently."

Imagine that response from a doctor treating a patient. Doctors, like teachers, do not always know the story behind the pain. They treat anyway. We should not need to KNOW about the source or nature of the trauma, or even if the behavior is a result of trauma, to be able to RESPOND effectively to kids in crisis.

The good news is, while trauma-informed practice is necessary for students experiencing trauma, it is good for everyone!

## --IT TAKES A VILLAGE--

Mrs. Ryan is a seasoned educator with a LOT of experience managing behavior. After all, she has been teaching first graders for twenty years! She has embraced the research and was willing to press forward even though at her school, she was a pioneer in this movement. Her choice to respond to Jayla's behavior as *a coping skill deficit* rather than react to it as *a discipline problem* will make a difference for Jayla. However, what will happen to Jayla when she moves on to second grade? If her future teachers engage in adult behaviors that are punitive and/or unpredictable, will Jayla be trapped in the stress-response cycle of hypervigilance and explosive behaviors again?

Christopher Blodgett, Director of the Washington State University, CLEAR Trauma Center. CLEAR (Collaborative Learning for Educational Achievement and Resiliency) is one of the front runners for implementing effective trauma-sensitive practices in schools. Blodgett's research makes it clear that, if we really want long-term change, it requires a shift in the behaviors of all adults on campus. "If your neighbor does not change his practice, it is not sustainable."[68] It is not sustainable for the adults doing it alone, as without support, adults will shift back into established habits. (Hence, the necessity for support groups like Alcoholics Anonymous or Weight Watchers). It is not sustainable for the kids if they are still in an unpredictable environment because there is not consensus between adults. It not only takes a village, but it takes a unified village to make such a drastic shift in educational practices.

On the other hand, imagine a school that embraces a shared vision of trauma-sensitive practices, a community where all adults respond to behavior with compassion, where children are supported and not punished for their inability to self-regulate and cope with stress, where children are taught how to self-manage instead of simply told their behavior is not acceptable. Imagine a school where all children are taught to support and care for one another.

Now imagine those children as adults.

Now imagine the community if all children, in all schools, had this environment.

*You are imagining possibility.*

## --FROM THE EXPERTS--

Given the prevalence of early childhood trauma among school-aged children, educators need strategies to help children overcome the negative effects of their early life experiences. Overall this means helping teachers appreciate the brain's never-ending plasticity- its capacity to change within the context of nurturing, social relationships... It is important for teachers to understand how persistent adversity weakens the brain's operating system as well as how healthy, stimulating school experiences can help children create compensatory strategies that allow them to reach their highest potential.

-Susan E. Craig[69]

"When young children experience a traumatic stressor, their first response is usually to look for reassurance from the adults who care for them... These adults can help reestablish security and stability for children who have experienced trauma."

-The National Child Traumatic Stress Network[70]

Trauma in the Classroom

# 12

# A Prescription for Healing

"It is easier to **BUILD**

**STRONG CHILDREN**

than to repair broken men."

–Frederick Douglass[71]

## --SYSTEM-WIDE PRESCRIPTION--

In order to get our education system in line to obtain our goal, we need to:

1. **INFORM ADMINISTRATORS, TEACHERS, SUPPORT STAFF** and all others working with students what trauma does to brain development. They need, *they deserve to* understand the neuroscience. They need to understand why our typical methods are not working. They need to know what will work.

2. **CHANGE OUR RESPONSE TO DISCIPLINE.** We must stop using punitive consequences as a sole disciplinary tactic if we expect the behavior to change. The problem is two-fold. We spend all our energy telling them what NOT to do, and they are never taught what to do instead. Additionally, when we send them home, we are contributing to their confusion and distress. If the home environment is stressful, we are sending them back to a stressful environment under stressful circumstances. Additionally, when parents are called at work to come and get their child due to behavior, it increases parent stress both at home and in the work place. They miss work (often without pay) and

often parents are also unable to cause a change in child behavior. This increases the stress at home, and adds to the cycle of toxic stress. We need to exhaust all efforts to keep these kids at school. It is not only supportive for the kids, it is supportive for the family. This cannot be done with traditional resources. Students are sent home because we lack resources necessary to maintain them safely on campus. Necessary supports cannot be neglected if this practice is going to change.

3. **PROVIDE ONGOING SUPPORT TO ADULTS** supporting these children. When I teach educators about the effects of trauma, close to 90% of teachers change their opinion of these students and their behavior. They shift from placing blame on student or parent to assuming responsibility for helping these kids in crisis. However, regardless of their immediate change, the results are not sustainable without ongoing support. Changing practices is difficult. It requires ongoing professional development opportunities, coaching, mentoring and guided self-reflection in order to maintain momentum and stamina. Trauma-sensitive practices require a change in adult behavior in order

to change student behavior. This cannot be done without adequate adult support.

4. **PROVIDE SAFE AND SUPPORTIVE ENVIRONMENT** for ALL students and staff. Current discipline practices exist because we are trying to keep our school environment safe. The problem is, it is then only safe when those students are not on campus. We need to provide an environment that can be safe when everyone is present. A supportive environment is one where all students feel safe, **even when they are in crisis**. A supportive environment is one that teaches students how to cope with their own crises, and then helps them through the crises that occur at school.

## --CLASSROOM PRESCRIPTION--

Our teachers are our first responders. In order for change to occur, we need to empower teachers. We need to give them resources they can use to avoid a crisis. We need to give them, not just a new tool, but an entire tool-box.

The experts all agree the key lies in the relationship between teacher and child, the teacher's ability to establish an environment that feels safe for all students, and the teacher's opportunity to teach students some simple stress management techniques. Here are a few simple techniques any teacher can begin using immediately.

1.  **TEACH THE WHOLE CLASS** that everyone feels stress. Teach them to identify how their body feels when they start to feel stress. Then teach them all a simple response such as "stop and breathe." Along with this strategy, teach them how they can help each other cope with stress. This will not only empower students to gain control of their own stress, but it will help non-stressed classmates feel a sense of control over their environment because they will know how to help their stressed peers.

2.  **ESTABLISH A SAFE TIME-OUT AREA IN THE CLASSROOM.** This is NOT to be confused with time-out as a consequence of behavior, but rather a time-out to *prevent* **stress-induced behavior**. Compare it to a time-out in a basketball or football game. Sometimes the player calls the time-out, sometimes the coach calls it. The purpose for the time-out is often to **stop** and come up with a plan to **gain control**. This is also the

103

purpose for a classroom time-out area. It is a place the student can go because he feels he needs it, or the teacher feels he needs it. The time-out is simply that: an opportunity to **stop** and come up with a plan to **gain control**. It is time away from the demands of the classroom. Time-outs in athletic events come with time constraints and limitations, so should classroom time-outs. However, those time constraints and limitations will vary by student. The teacher needs to come up with an individual plan that increases the likelihood of success for the students who need that option.

3. **MAKE TIME TO BUILD RELATIONSHIPS.** One strategy that I often recommend teachers use is the 2 x 10 strategy published in The Cornerstone for Teachers. The 2 x 10 strategy is this: spend 2 minutes per day for at least 10 days in a row simply talking with an at-risk student.[72] There are two rules for this conversation. 1) Do not address behavior! It is not possible to build a relationship with someone by bringing up all their negative behavior in every conversation. The at-risk student needs desperately to make a connection

with an adult. If connecting only occurs when behavior is severe or disruptive, the student behavior may escalate in an attempt to establish that connection. It is critical for the adult to make it a point to have *at least one intentional conversation per day* that steers clear of behavior. 2) The topic of conversation is entirely up to the student. If he wants to talk about mud, talk about mud. Let him pick the topic. You may set parameters for the conversation, but exercise caution with censorship. If the student is censored, it can increase his stress (fear of saying the wrong thing) and prevent him from being open and honest. His ability to be honest will increase his confidence in the relationship. If the student picks a terribly inappropriate topic, or uses undesirable language, you can teach "Time and Place." (See #5)

4.  **DEVELOP A SIGNAL** the student can use to let you know she needs help pulling it together. Mrs. Ryan used a hug with Jayla, but there are lots of different cues you can use. Teach the student to use the signal BEFORE she loses control. When a student is given a signal to use, it is crucial for

the teacher to respond to the signal. That is the key to maintaining student trust. The signal should be age appropriate, school appropriate, and something that is meaningful to the student.

5. **TEACH TIME AND PLACE.** It is crucial for kids to develop a sense of connectedness to their school community. Unfortunately, when kids are told all day long that their behavior is inappropriate, we are creating a separation, not a connection. The way a person acts is a reflection of their "normal." If we tell them their normal is inappropriate or unacceptable, they will never want a relationship with us. Rather than telling kids their behavior is inappropriate altogether, teach them *time and place*. There is a time and a place for everything. This is pretty simple and is easily done whole group. Get the kids involved with talking about how they act in different environments such as the park, the movies, the grocery store, grandma's house, or church, then talk about how we act at school. The idea is to draw out their prior knowledge of the concept of "time and place" and use that to our advantage. We can then teach them that school requires a certain behavior, and

different <u>places</u> on campus allow for different behaviors. It is okay to run on the playground, but it is important to walk in the halls. Additionally, different <u>times</u> require different behavior. While it is okay to run and yell on the field most of the time, during a fire drill, it is necessary to walk quietly and stay with the class. When children understand the concept of time and place, it is much easier for them to adapt to new environments with different expectations. This also makes it easy for the teacher to correct the behavior without leaving the student feeling judged. "Max, school is not the place for _____. Now is the time for _____." Corrective feedback given- student dignity preserved.

Trauma in the Classroom

# 13

## BE THE DIFFERENCE

"YOU CANNOT GO THROUGH A SINGLE DAY WITHOUT HAVING AN IMPACT ON THE WORLD AROUND YOU.

**WHAT** YOU DO **MAKES A DIFFERENCE**

AND YOU HAVE TO DECIDE WHAT KIND OF DIFFERENCE **YOU** WANT TO MAKE."

–JANE GOODALL[73]

## --EARLY INTERVENTION--

Early intervention is paramount for these kids. While research is telling us that the brain undergoes change all the way until death, it also shows us that tremendous healing and repair can occur when we intervene, and intervene intensively, *while kids are young.* The problem is, we are often afraid to intervene aggressively. We wait around to see if it will improve over time.

What if the E.R. doctor waited around to see if my heart-attack improved over time? Or tried a less invasive intervention first, such as a few hours of aspirin alone? This simply does not happen because we recognize, collectively, the importance of aggressive intervention to treat urgent conditions. We know that early and effective intervention will increase our ability to prevent permanent damage to the heart, and even death.

When students are experiencing toxic stress, intervention at an early age is critical; urgency is essential. Childhood development specialists have identified a window of time where children learn to manage their feelings. Judith Graham, human development specialist, reports, "Emotions develop in layers, each more complex than the last. The stress response develops immediately, from birth through age 3; empathy and envy begin to develop during the second year through about age 10."[74] Without guidance and support, these feelings remain misunderstood and mismanaged.

Harvard's Center on the Developing Child, among other leading experts, recommends early intervention. "The basic principles of neuroscience indicate that **early preventive intervention** will be more efficient and produce more favorable outcomes than remediation later in life."[75]

Jayla was six when Mrs. Ryan started to intervene. Her process of repair began almost immediately. The longer a child is exposed to adversity without appropriate support, without learning stress-management, self-regulation and appropriate coping mechanisms, the longer it will take for the repair to be evident.

## --THE BIGGER PICTURE--

Teachers are not therapists. While there are steps they can take to increase the success of all students in their classroom, they cannot solve the bigger issue. The problem runs much deeper than the classroom disruptions, and the solution needs to be much broader than changing some practices in schools. Chris Blodgett said, "Schools are reflections of the community they are in."[76] We have a mounting body of evidence that the population of students in crisis is growing. As a reflection of the community, this means we also have a growing population of families in crisis.

I do not believe for one minute that most instances of childhood adversity occur because a parent chooses to create an environment of overwhelm for their child: quite the contrary. I am confident that the majority of parents want their children to be happy, calm and successful. I doubt you will find any parent who will say they want their child to live in a constant state of fear and confusion. ***Trauma presents in our children as a result of parents or caregivers who are also in distress.*** Wanting what is best for their child does not mean they have the tools to provide it. ***Trauma is often generational.*** Many of the parents of our children in distress also experienced chronic adversity during childhood. ***Trauma is also circumstantial and environmental.*** Certain circumstances limit access to resources and increase the distress of the family. Environmental conditions can do the same.

Repairing practices in the school is only a piece of the puzzle; there is much more work to do. This is a community issue and it is time to take charge of our communities. Families need to be strengthened. Schools can help with this. The school, after all, is the common tie within the community. While educators are not therapists, they are educators. Healing the community requires educating the community as much as it requires a change in the way we, as educators, respond to children in distress.

It can be done **because we are the village.**

Together, **WE** can heal our communities.

## --FROM THE EXPERTS--

"Intervention is likely to be more effective and less costly when it is provided earlier in life rather than later."

-The National Early Childhood Technical Assistance Center[77]

"All sectors of society need to be well informed about the relationships between severe stress and trauma and an individual's success in their lives, their health, their productivity."

–David Corwin, MD[78]

"In the words of Dr. Robert Block, the former President of the American Academy of Pediatrics, 'Adverse childhood experiences are the single greatest public health threat facing our nation today.'"

–Nadine Burke Harris[79]

# 14

# A CALL TO ACTION

I SHALL BE TELLING THIS WITH A SIGH

SOMEWHERE AGES AND AGES HENCE:

TWO ROADS DIVERGED IN A WOOD, AND I-

I TOOK THE ONE LESS TRAVELED BY,

AND **THAT** HAS **MADE** ALL **THE DIFFERENCE**.

-Robert Frost[80]

## --THE ROAD LESS TRAVELED--

We are in a position to choose the path that will make all the difference. Thomas Suddendorf, professor of psychology at the University of Queensland, and author of *The Gap: The Science of What Separates Us from Other Animals*, stated, "Humans seem to rely on a uniquely flexible way to control behavior through clever thinking. We can use our capacity to think about alternative situations…. We can compare alternative routes to the future and deliberately select one plan over another…"[81]

In other words, the very thing that separates us from the rest of the animal kingdom is our ability to ***make informed decisions*** and ***change our behavior***. As adults, it is our responsibility to nurture the next generation. When science provides us evidence that supports necessary change in order to effectively nurture, **we must act.**

The science is clear. Chronic, toxic stress during early childhood development changes the way the brain perceives and responds to information. The research is consistent. Sociologists, psychologists, social workers, counselors, and educators have found our traditional attempts to support learning and change the behavior of these students inadequate, and even damaging. They are also finding that when **WE** change our response from punitive to compassionate and when we teach kids how to manage their stress, repair, healing, ***and then learning***, are all possible.

## --A CALL TO ACTION--

When biological science and social science perfectly align in their findings, we need to act. Remember what Suddendorf said: "We can use our capacity to think about alternative situations… We can compare alternative routes to the future and ***deliberately select one plan over another…***"

Education is at a crossroad. We need to choose between routes. Based on science, extensive research, and statistics derived from current practices that are failing, we know what the future holds if we deliberately continue to choose our current course.

***It is time to change the future.***

It is time to choose a different road.

Trauma in the Classroom

# Postscript
## WHAT HAPPENED TO JAYLA?

### "BE THE CHANGE

YOU WANT TO

SEE IN THE WORLD."

-MAHATMA GANDHI[82]

## --FINISHING FIRST GRADE--

Mrs. Ryan reported that Jayla finished first grade in control. Once "stop and breathe" was introduced, she never returned to "The Hulk" and classroom evacuations were no longer necessary. She would still sometimes growl, but she would also sometimes sing: she was rarely quiet, but she did stop screaming and crying. Mrs. Ryan established a calming place for Jayla to go if she needed time away from the class, and Jayla knew she could access that space without fear of consequence. Jayla's behavior improved so much, other adults on campus recognized it.

Mrs. Ryan still had to modify assignments in order to make sure Jayla could be successful, but ultimately, Jayla was able to get some work done. Jayla was especially proud of herself when she completed the same math test as her peers and scored 75%. She was very proud of her solid C grade. And deservedly so, Jayla had to work harder than her classmates to get to a place where learning could begin. Mrs. Ryan was also very proud of that solid C grade. After all, she worked harder to give Jayla the support she needed to get to a place where learning could begin. Mrs. Ryan did not wait for change; she became the change.

Be the change YOU want to see in the world.

"NEVER **BELIEVE**

**THAT** A FEW

**CARING PEOPLE** CAN'T

**CHANGE**

**THE WORLD.**

FOR, INDEED,

THAT'S ALL WHO EVER HAVE."

–MARGARET MEAD [83]

**Stacey Sly**

## About The Author

Stacey Sly is a Behavior Interventionist.  Although it is her profession, she has also made it her personal mission to actively advocate for children experiencing the adverse effects of trauma.

Sly and her husband fostered nine children over seven years.  As a foster parent, she learned through first-hand experience just how much severe adversity impacts childhood development.  As a behavior interventionist in the schools, she sees the direct impact to learning.

She is an advocate for implementing educational policies that address the needs of these kids, and believes strongly that teachers can be empowered to support the healing and repair process.

She is also tackling this issue as a community issue, not just a school issue.

Sly has her Bachelor of Arts and a Master of Science degree in Special Education, as well as a Master of Science degree in Educational Leadership.

She has seven children *(through birth and adoption)* and two grandchildren.

It is her dream to be part of a community where ALL children have ***opportunity.***

*...**opportunity to live happily ever after.***

# Recommended Resources

Burke Harris, N.  (2014): *How childhood trauma affects health across a lifetime.* TEDMED. Retrieved from https://www.ted.com/talks/nadine_burke_harris_ho w_childhood_trauma_affects_health_across_a_lifeti me?language=en

Cole, Susan, Greenwald Obrien, Jessica, Gadd, M. Geron, et. al. (2005, 2009*). Helping Traumatized Children Learn. Supportive school environments for children traumatized by family violence. A Report and Policy Agenda.* Massachusetts Advocates for Children: Trauma and Learning Policy Initiative in collaboration with Harvard Law School and The Task Force on Children Affected by Domestic Violence.

Craig, Susan E. (2016). Trauma-Sensitive Schools LEARNING COMMUNITIES TRANSFORMING CHILDREN'S LIVES, K-5. Teachers College Press New York, NY.

Forbes, Heather T. 2012: *Help for Billy.* Boulder, CO. Beyond Consequences Institute, LLC.

Forbes, T. & Post, B. (2009). Beyond Consequences, Logic, and Control: A Love Based Approach to Helping Children With Severe Behavior. (Vol 1). Boulder, Co: Beyond Consequences Institute; LLC.

Howard, J. (2013). Distressed or Deliberately Defiant?: Managing challenging student behavior due to trauma and disorganized attachment. Toowong QLD, Australia: Australian Academic Press.

Kauffman, D. (2015). Childhood trauma is the elephant in the classroom. Children's Mental Health Network shaping the story... Retrieved from http://www.cmhnetwork.org/media-center/morning-zen/childhood-trauma-is-the-elephant-in-the-classroom

Medina, J. (2014). brain rules: 12 Principles for Surviving and Thriving at Work, Home and School. (2nd ed.). Seattle, WA: Pear Press.

Watson, Angela, *2 x 10 Strategy: a miraculous solution for behavior issues?* Retrieved from http://thecornerstoneforteachers.com/2014/10/the-2x10-strategy-a-miraculous-solution-for-behavior-issues.html

# References

Blackney, Victoria. (2016). *The Prevalence of Violence and Trauma in Nevada.* Supporting Student Resiliency in Trauma-Sensitive Schools. Reno, NV

Blodgett, Christopher (2016). *Aces to Action.* Supporting Student Resilience in Trauma-Sensitive Schools. Reno, Nevada.

Bradbury, T. (2015) *9 Things That Make Good Employees Quit.* TALENTSMART. Retrieved from http://www.talentsmart.com/articles/9-Things-That-Make-Good-Employees-Quit-172420765-p-1.html

Burke Harris, N. (2014): *How childhood trauma affects health across a lifetime.* TEDMED. Retrieved from https://www.ted.com/talks/nadine_burke_harris_ho w_childhood_trauma_affects_health_across_a_lifeti me?language=en

Center on the Developing Child. (2015). I*nBrief: Early Childhood Mental Health.* Cambridge, MA: Harvard University. Retrieved from http://developingchild.harvard.edu/index.php/activit ies/council/

Centers for Disease Control. (2014). Injury Prevention & Control: Division of Violence Prevention. ACES Study. Retrieved from http://www.cdc.gov/ violenceprevention/acestudy/index.html

Craig, K. (2015). *Dealing with "Difficult" Students: Compilation of the 5-Week Series.* PULSE. Retrieved from https://www.linkedin.com/pulse/dealing-difficult-students-compilation-5-week-series-kathryn-craig

Coffroth, Megan. (2013). *Things We Can Still Learn from Dr. Seuss.* Retrieved from https://megancoffroth.wordpress.com/2013/06/17/things-we-can-still-learn-from-dr-seuss/

Cole, Susan, Greenwald Obrien, Jessica, Gadd, M. Geron, et. al. (2005, 2009*). Helping Traumatized Children Learn. Supportive school environments for children traumatized by family violence. A Report and Policy Agenda.* Massachusetts Advocates for Children: Trauma and Learning Policy Initiative in collaboration with Harvard Law School and The Task Force on Children Affected by Domestic Violence.

Corwin, David. MD (2015). *The Adverse Childhood Experiences Study.* Joscelyn Hill; Scott Henderson; Dan Allen. Retrieved from https://www.youtube.com/watch?v=IbsXh6wwc3Q&ebc=ANyPxKqslFlIFec2wwlkGjU2Ye5RdPM4nXB_thRgKXoWeaDsA95YMVwM5UbsH0UheCd1hGnNhtsUcPjTg3KibNypWbpRstbg

Craig, Susan E. (2016). Trauma-Sensitive Schools LEARNING COMMUNITIES TRANSFORMING CHILDREN'S LIVES, K-5. Teachers College Press New York, NY.

Forbes, Heather T. 2012: *Help for Billy*. Boulder, CO.
Beyond Consequences Institute, LLC.

Forbes, T. & Post, B. (2009). Beyond Consequences,
Logic, and Control: A Love Based Approach to
Helping Children With Severe Behavior. (Vol 1).
Boulder, Co: Beyond Consequences Institute; LLC.

Goodreads. (2016). *Frederick Douglass. Quotable Quote.*
Retrieved from
http://www.goodreads.com/quotes/28899-it-is-
easier-to-build-strong-children-than-to-repair

Goodreads. (2016). *Jane Goodall. Quotable Quote.*
Retrieved from http://www.goodreads.com
/quotes/159740-what-you-do-makes-a-difference-
and-you-have-to

Goodreads. (2016). Mahatma Gandhi. Quotable Quotes.
Retrieved from
http://www.goodreads.com/quotes/24499-be-the-
change-that-you-wish-to-see-in-the

Gordon, Dani. (2015). *Bedside manner trumps quality
care: 8 stats on American's physician preference.*
Becker's Hospital Review. Retrieved from
http://www.beckershospitalreview.com/hospital-
physician-relationships/bedside-manner-trumps-
quality-care-8-stats-on-americans-physician-
preference.html

Howard, J. (2013). Distressed or Deliberately Defiant?:
    Managing challenging student behavior due to
    trauma and disorganized attachment. Toowong
    QLD, Australia: Australian Academic Press.

Johns Hopkins University, 2010: *Center for Mental Health
    Services in Pediatric Primary Care*. Retrieved
    from www.nctsn.org.

Frost, Robert. (1920). *The Road Not Taken.* Mountain
    Interval. Retrieved from
    http://www.bartleby.com/119/1.html

Graham, J. (2001. 2011). *Children and Brain Development:
    What We Know About How Children Learn.*
    Cooperative Extension Publications. Bulletin
    #4356. Retrieved from
    https://extension.umaine.edu/publications/4356e/

Kauffman, D. (2015). Childhood trauma is the elephant in
    the classroom. Children's Mental Health Network
    shaping the story... Retrieved from
    http://www.cmhnetwork.org/media-center/morning-
    zen/childhood-trauma-is-the-elephant-in-the-
    classroom

Levy, Leah. (2014). *How Stress Affects the Brain During
    Learning.* Edudemic connecting education &
    technology. Retrieved from
    http://www.edudemic.com/stress-affects-brain-
    learning/

Loudenback, J. (2016). *The 'Silent Epidemic' of Child Trauma.* The Chronicle of Social Change. Retrieved from https://chronicleofsocialchange.org/los-angeles/child-trauma-as-a-silent-epidemic/16869

Medina, J. (2014). brain rules: 12 Principles for Surviving and Thriving at Work, Home and School. (2$^{nd}$ ed.). Seattle, WA: Pear Press.

Peifer, Angie. (2014). *The Purpose of Public Education and the Role of the School Board.* National School Boards Association. National Connection. Retrieved From http://www.nsba.org/sites/default/files/The%20Purpose%20of%20Public%20Education%20and%20the%20Role%20of%20the%20School%20Board_National%20Connection.pdf

Primary Sources. (2012). *AMERICA'S TEACHERS ON THE TEACHING PROFESSION: A Project of Scholastic and the Bill & Melinda Gates Foundation.* Retrieved from http://www.scholastic.com/primarysources/pdfs/Gates2012_full.pdf

Ryst, Erika (2016). *What Does Trauma Look Like in Nevada Schools? A Clinical Perspective.* Supporting Student Resilience in Trauma-Sensitive Schools. Reno, Nevada

Sporleder, Jim as quoted by Worth, Tammy. (2015). *Taking A Different Approach To Behavioral Problems In School: 'Trauma-Informed" Care.* Retrieved from http://kcur.org/post/taking-different-approach-behavioral-problems-school-trauma-informed-care#stream/0

Sprouts Development. (2015). @SproutsDevpmt. Knost, L.R. Retrieved from https://twitter.com/sproutsdevpmt/status/627671180657340417

Stevens, J. (2014). *To prevent childhood trauma, pediatricians screen children and their parents...and sometimes, just parents...for childhood trauma.* ACES Too High News. Retrieved from https://acestoohigh.com/2014/07/29/to-prevent-childhood-trauma-pediatricians-screen-children-and-their-parentsand-sometimes-just-parents/

Stevens, J. (January 28, 2014). *San Francisco's El Dorado Elementary uses trauma-informed & restorative practices; suspensions drop 89%.* ACES Too High. Retrieved from http://acestoohigh.com/2014/01/28/hearts-el-dorado-elementary/.

Suddendorf, T. (2014). *What sets us apart from the animals?* ABC. AU. Retrieved from http://www.abc.net.au/radionational/programs/ockhamsrazor/5303368

The National Child Traumatic Stress Network. (2016). Retrieved from www.NCTSN.org

The National Early Childhood Technical Assistance
　　　Center. (2011). *The Importance of Early
　　　Intervention for Infants and Toddlers with
　　　Disabilities and their Families.* Retrieved from
　　　http://www.nectac.org/~pdfs/pubs/importanceofearl
　　　yintervention.pdf

Watson, Angela, *2 x 10 Strategy: a miraculous solution for
　　　behavior issues?* Retrieved from
　　　http://thecornerstoneforteachers.com/2014/10/the-
　　　2x10-strategy-a-miraculous-solution-for-behavior-
　　　issues.html

Wisdom Quotes. (2016). Retrieved from
　　　wisdomquotes.com/quote/African-proverb.html

Worth, Tammy. (2015). *Taking A Different Approach To
　　　Behavioral Problems In School: 'Trauma-
　　　Informed' Care.* Retrieved from
　　　http://kcur.org/post/taking-different-approach-
　　　behavioral-problems-school-trauma-informed-
　　　care#stream/0

Zero to Six Collaborative Group, The National Child
　　　Traumatic Stress Network. (2010). *Early Childhood
　　　Trauma.* Los Angeles, CA & Durham, NC:
　　　National Center for Child Traumatic Stress.

## Notes

[1] Goodreads. (2016). Mahatma Gandhi. Quotable Quotes. Retrieved from http://www.goodreads.com/quotes/24499-be-the-change-that-you-wish-to-see-in-the

[2] Burke Harris, N. (2014): *How childhood trauma affects health across a lifetime.* TEDMED. Retrieved from https://www.ted.com/talks/nadine_burke_harris_how_child hood_trauma_affects_health_across_a_lifetime?language=e n

[3] Sporleder, Jim as quoted by Worth, Tammy. (2015). *Taking A Different Approach To Behavioral Problems In School: 'Trauma-Informed" Care.* Retrieved from http://kcur.org/post/taking-different-approach-behavioral-problems-school-trauma-informed-care#stream/0

[4] Burke Harris, N. (2014): (As in n.2 above).

[5] Burke Harris, N. (2014): (As in n.2 above).

[6] Kauffman, D. (2015). *Childhood trauma is the elephant in the classroom.* Children's Mental Health Network shaping the story… Retrieved from http://www.cmhnetwork.org/media-center/morning-zen/childhood-trauma-is-the-elephant-in-the-classroom

[7] Burke Harris, N. (2014). (As in n. 2 above).

[8] Craig, K. (2015). *Dealing with "Difficult" Students: Compilation of the 5-Week Series.* PULSE. Retrieved from https://www.linkedin.com/pulse/dealing-difficult-students-compilation-5-week-series-kathryn-craig

[9] Burke Harris, N. 2014: (As in n.2 above).

[10] Forbes, Heather T. 2012: *Help for Billy.* Boulder, CO. Beyond Consequences Institute, LLC.

Johns Hopkins University, 2010: *Center for Mental Health Services in Pediatric Primary Care.* Retrieved from www.nctsn.org.

[11] Forbes, Heather T. 2012: (As in 10 above).

[12] Blodgett, Christopher (2016). *Aces to Action.* Supporting Student Resilience in Trauma-Sensitive Schools. Reno, Nevada

[13] Corwin, David. MD (2015). *The Adverse Childhood Experiences Study.* Joscelyn Hill; Scott Henderson; Dan Allen. Retrieved from https://www.youtube.com/watch?v=IbsXh6wwc3Q&ebc= ANyPxKqslFlIFec2wwlkGjU2Ye5RdPM4nXB_thRgKX-poWeaDsA95YMVwM5UbsH0UheCd1hGnNhtsUcPjTg3 KibNypWbpRstbg

[14] Cole, Susan, Greenwald Obrien, Jessica, Gadd, M. Geron, et. al. (2005, 2009*). Helping Traumatized Children Learn. Supportive school environments for children traumatized by family violence. A Report and Policy Agenda.* Massachusetts Advocates for Children: Trauma and Learning Policy Initiative in collaboration with Harvard Law School and The Task Force on Children Affected by Domestic Violence.

[15] Levy, Leah. (2014). *How Stress Affects the Brain During Learning.* Edudemic connecting education & technology. Retrieved from http://www.edudemic.com/stress-affects-brain-learning/

[16] Center on the Developing Child. (2015). *InBrief: Early Childhood Mental Health.* Cambridge, MA: Harvard University. Retrieved from http://developingchild.harvard.edu/index.php/activities/council/

[17] Medina, J. (2014). *brain rules: 12 Principles for Surviving and Thriving at Work, Home and School.* (2nd ed.). Seattle, WA: Pear Press.

[18] Burke Harris, N. (2014): (As in n.2 above).

[19] Forbes, T. & Post, B. (2009). *Beyond Consequences, Logic, and Control: A Love Based Approach to Helping Children With Severe Behavior.* (Vol 1). Boulder, Co: Beyond Consequences Institute; LLC.

[20] Howard, J. (2013). *Distressed or Deliberately Defiant?: Managing challenging student behavior due to trauma and disorganized attachment.* Toowong QLD, Australia: Australian Academic Press.

[21] Craig, Susan E. (2016). *Trauma-Sensitive Schools LEARNING COMMUNITIES TRANSFORMING CHILDREN'S LIVES, K-5.* Teachers College Press New York, NY.

[22] Stevens, J. (2014). *To prevent childhood trauma, pediatricians screen children and their parents...and sometimes, just parents...for childhood trauma.* ACES Too High News. Retrieved from https://acestoohigh.com/2014/07/29/to-prevent-childhood-trauma-pediatricians-screen-children-and-their-parentsand-sometimes-just-parents/

[23] Canty Graves, J. & Graves C. (2016*). Response to Intervention Falls Short. Parents Have The Power TO Make Special Education Work.* Retrieved from http://www.makespecialeducationwork.com/response-intervention-falls-short-2/#sthash.DVCN7NbT.DnKAAVmO.dpbs.

[24] The National Child Traumatic Stress Network. (2008). *Child Trauma Toolkit for Educators.* Retrieved from http://rems.ed.gov/docs/NCTSN_ChildTraumaToolkitForEducators.pdf

[25] Advanced Learning Institute (2009). *The Incubation Stage of Learning.* Cracking the Learning Code. Retrieved from http://crackingthelearningcode.com/element-28/

[26] Forbes, Heather T. 2012: (As in 10 above).

[27] Craig, Susan E. (2016). (As in n. 21 above)

[28] Medina, John (2014). (As in n. 17 above).

[29] Wong, H. (2005). *The First Days of School: How to Be an Effective Teacher.* Harry K. Wong Publications. Mountain View, CA.

[30] Public Agenda. (2004). *Teaching Interrupted: Do Discipline Policies in Today's Public Schools Foster the Common Good?* Retrieved from www.publicagenda.org.

[31] Public Agenda. (2004). (As in n. 30 above)

[32] Primary Sources. (2012). *AMERICA'S TEACHERS ON THE TEACHING PROFESSION: A Project of Scholastic and the Bill & Melinda Gates Foundation.* Retrieved from

http://www.scholastic.com/primarysources/pdfs/Gates2012
_full.pdf


[33] Medina, J. (2014). (As in n. 17 above)

[34] Cole, Susan, Greenwald Obrien, Jessica, Gadd, M.
Geron, et. al. (2005, 2009). (As in n.14 above)


[35] Forbes, T. & Post, B. (2009). (As in n. 19 above)

[36] Howard, J. (2013). (As in n. 20 above)


[37] McLeod, S. A. (2016). *Bandura - Social Learning
Theory*. Retrieved from
www.simplypsychology.org/bandura.html

[38] Stevens, J. (2012). *The adverse childhood experiences
study. The most important public health study you never
heard of- began in an obesity clinic.* ACES Too High
News. Retrieved from
https://acestoohigh.com/2012/10/03/the-adverse-childhood-
experiences-study-the-largest-most-important-public-
health-study-you-never-heard-of-began-in-an-obesity-
clinic/

[39] Cole, Susan; Eisner, Anne; Gregory, Michael; Ristuccia,
Joel. (2013). (As in n. 47 above).

[40] Worth, Tammy. (2015). *Taking A Different Approach To
Behavioral Problems In School: 'Trauma-Informed' Care.*
Retrieved from http://kcur.org/post/taking-different-
approach-behavioral-problems-school-trauma-informed-
care#stream/0

[41] The National Child Traumatic Stress Network. (2016). Retrieved from www.NCTSN.org

[42] Craig, Susan E. (2016). (As in n. 21 above)

[43] https://en.wikipedia.org/wiki/Law_of_the_instrument

[44] Howard, J. (2013). (As in n. 20 above)

[45] Forbes, Heather T. 2012: (As in 10 above).

[46] Longert., Sharon. (2016). *Teacher Behavior/ Student Behavior*. Teachers network. Retrieved from http://www.teachersnetwork.org/ntol/howto/adjust/behavior.htm

[47] Cole, Susan; Eisner, Anne; Gregory, Michael; Ristuccia, Joel. (2013). *Helping Traumatized Children Learn. V2. Safe, supportive learning environments that benefit all children. Creating and Advocating for Trauma-Sensitive Schools.* Trauma and Learning Policy Initiative a partnership of Massachusetts Advocates for Children and Harvard Law School.

[48] Loudenback, J. (2016). *The 'Silent Epidemic' of Child Trauma.* The Chronicle of Social Change. Retrieved from https://chronicleofsocialchange.org/los-angeles/child-trauma-as-a-silent-epidemic/16869

[49] Coffroth, Megan. (2013). *Things We Can Still Learn from Dr. Seuss.* Retrieved from https://megancoffroth.wordpress.com/2013/06/17/things-we-can-still-learn-from-dr-seuss/

[50] Center on the Developing Child. (2015). *InBrief: Early Childhood Mental Health.* Cambridge, MA: Harvard University. Retrieved from http://developingchild.harvard.edu/index.php/activities/council/

[51] Peifer, Angie. (2014). *The Purpose of Public Education and the Role of the School Board.* National School Boards Association. National Connection. Retrieved from http://www.nsba.org/sites/default/files/The%20Purpose%20of%20Public%20Education%20and%20the%20Role%20of%20the%20School%20Board_National%20Connection.pdf

[52] Craig, Susan E. (2016). (As in n. 21 above)

[53] Loudenback, J. (2016). (as in n. 48 above).

[54] Blodgett, Christopher (2016). (As in n.12 above).

[55] Ryst, Erika (2016). *What Does Trauma Look Like in Nevada Schools? A Clinical Perspective.* Supporting Student Resilience in Trauma-Sensitive Schools. Reno, Nevada

[56] Blodgett, Christopher (2016). (As in n.12 above).

[57] Sprouts Development. (2015). @SproutsDevpmt. Knost, L.R. Retrieved from https://twitter.com/sproutsdevpmt/status/627671180657340417

[58] Gordon, Dani. (2015). *Bedside manner trumps quality care: 8 stats on American's physician preference.* Becker's Hospital Review. Retrieved from http://www.beckershospitalreview.com/hospital-physician-

relationships/bedside-manner-trumps-quality-care-8-stats-on-americans-physician-preference.html

[59] Bradbury, T. (2015) *9 Things That Make Good Employees Quit*. TALENTSMART. Retrieved from http://www.talentsmart.com/articles/9-Things-That-Make-Good-Employees-Quit-172420765-p-1.html

[60] Forbes, Heather T. 2012: (As in 10 above). *Emphasis added.*

[61] Stevens, J. (January 28, 2014). *San Francisco's El Dorado Elementary uses trauma-informed & restorative practices; suspensions drop 89%.* ACES Too High. Retrieved from http://acestoohigh.com/2014/01/28/hearts-el-dorado-elementary/. *Emphasis added.*

[62] Blackney, Victoria. (2016). *The Prevalance of Violence and Trauma in Nevada.* Supporting Student Resiliency in Trauma-Sensitive Schools. Reno, NV

[63] Stephensen, Travis; Facebook. 2016. Retrieved from https://www.facebook.com/search/top/?q=travis%20stephensen%20posts

[64] Purtle, J. (2012). *How to turn 'What's wrong with you?' into 'What happened to you?'* The Public's Health. Retrieved from http://www.philly.com/philly/blogs/public_health/How-to-turn-Whats-wrong-with-you-into-What-happened-to-you.html

[65] Forbes, Heather T. 2012: (As in 10 above).

[66] Centers for Disease Control. (2014). Injury Prevention & Control: Division of Violence Prevention. ACES Study. Retrieved from

http://www.cdc.gov/violenceprevention/acestudy/index.html

[67] Wisdom Quotes. (2016). Retrieved from wisdomquotes.com/quote/African-proverb.html

[68] Blodgett, Christopher (2016). (As in n.12 above).

[69] Craig, Susan E. (2016). (As in n. 21 above)

[70] Zero to Six Collaborative Group, The National Child Traumatic Stress Network. (2010). *Early Childhood Trauma.* Los Angeles, CA & Durham, NC: National Center for Child Traumatic Stress.

[71] Goodreads. (2016). *Frederick Douglass. Quotable Quote.* Retrieved from http://www.goodreads.com/quotes/28899-it-is-easier-to-build-strong-children-than-to-repair

[72] Watson, Angela, *2 x 10 Strategy: a miraculous solution for behavior issues?* Retrieved from http://thecornerstoneforteachers.com/2014/10/the-2x10-strategy-a-miraculous-solution-for-behavior-issues.html

[73] Goodreads. (2016). *Jane Goodall. Quotable Quote.* Retrieved from http://www.goodreads.com/quotes/159740-what-you-do-makes-a-difference-and-you-have-to

[74] Graham, J. (2001. 2011). *Children and Brain Development: What We Know About How Children Learn.* Cooperative Extension Publications. Bulletin #4356. Retrieved from https://extension.umaine.edu/publications/4356e/

[75] Center on the Developing Child. (2007). *The Science of Early Childhood Development* (InBrief). Retrieved from www.developingchild.harvard.edu

[76] Blodgett, Christopher (2016). (As in n.12 above).

[77] The National Early Childhood Technical Assistance Center. (2011). *The Importance of Early Intervention for Infants and Toddlers with Disabilities and their Families.* Retrieved from http://www.nectac.org/~pdfs/pubs/importanceofearlyinterv ention.pdf

[78] Corwin, David, MD. (2015). (As in n. 13 above).

[79] Burke Harris, N. (2014): (As in n.2 above).

[80] Frost, Robert. (1920). *The Road Not Taken.* Mountain Interval. Retrieved from http://www.bartleby.com/119/1.html

[81] Suddendorf, T. (2014). *What sets us apart from the animals?* ABC. AU. Retreived from http://www.abc.net.au/radionational/programs/ockhamsrazr /5303368

[82] Goodreads. (2016). Mahatma Gandhi. Quotable Quotes. Retrieved from http://www.goodreads.com/quotes/24499- be-the-change-that-you-wish-to-see-in-the

[83] Mead, Margaret. (n.d.). BrainyQuote.com. Retrieved July 12, 2016 from http://brainyquote.com/quotes/quotes/ m/margaretme101283.html

CPSIA information can be obtained
at www.ICGtesting.com
Printed in the USA
LVHW031755011019
632856LV00010B/880/P